L   E COL ECE   T ND DESIGN

Skull

1994

woven tapestry

cotton warp, linen, wool and cotton weft

26 x 19cm (10 x 8in)

Illustrated artwork © Kay Lawrence AM
Essays © Dr Diana Wood Conroy &
Christopher Menz
Series Editor: Matthew Koumis
Reprographics: Ermanno Beverari
Printed in Italy by Grafiche AZ

© **Telos Art Publishing** 2002

Telos Art Publishing
PO Box 125, Winchester
SO23 7UJ, England
T   +44 (0) 1962 864546
F   +44 (0) 1962 864727
E   editorial@telos.net
E   sales@telos.net
W www.arttextiles.com

ISBN 1 902015 28 2 (softback)
ISBN 1 902015 44 4 (hardback)

A CIP catalogue record for this book is
available from The British Library

Notes
all dimensions are shown in metric and
imperial, height x width x depth

Photo Credits
Michal Kluvanek and Grant Hancock

Artist's Acknowledgements
'The Centenary of Women's Suffrage
Community Tapestries' (p29) was woven
by the Adelaide Community Weavers,
coordinator Elaine Gardner, Assistant
Lucia Pichler. Lucia Pichler also assisted
me in weaving 'From Italowie to
Chambers Gorge' (p20). 'Red Gorge,
Two Views' (p19) was woven by myself
with Jude Stewart, Chris Cocius, and
Shirley Benlow, with additional assistance
from Sue Rosenthal.

I also acknowledge with gratitude the
generous support of the following
institutions, whose assistance has
enabled production of the work
illustrated in this book: The South
Australian School of Art, University of
South Australia; The Canberra School of
Art, Australian National University; The
Faculty of Creative Arts, University of
Wollongong; The Government of South
Australia through ArtsSA; The Australia
Council.

Last but not least, I would like to thank
my family and friends for their patience,
good humour and sustaining
companionship over the years.

UNIVERSITY OF SOUTH AUSTRALIA

portfolio collection
Kay Lawrence

TELOS

Contents

Cup (detail of **Rust**)
2001

left:
Red Gorge, Two Views (detail)
1987-8
Collection of Parliament House,
Canberra

Foreword

For most Australians, and for many visitors to Australia, their first knowledge of Kay Lawrence's work is the vast embroidery in Parliament House, Canberra. The embroidery's technical skill, beauty, scale and scheme of images relating to Australian history and culture are equally admired. Sixteen metres in length, and involving a team of almost 500 embroiderers throughout Australia, the embroidery was designed and its production coordinated by Lawrence during 1983 to 1988. This huge work was commissioned for the new Parliament House (opened 1988) and is Lawrence's biggest and most complex project.

The technique of the Canberra work is embroidery, although Lawrence is principally a tapestry artist, her textile medium of choice. Tapestry-weaving in Australia is limited to a small group of practitioners, many of whom were influenced by the international interest in hand-woven textiles, and in the crafts generally, which burgeoned in this country during the 1970s.

Although some weavers in Australia follow the long-established historical precedent of adapting paintings by well-known artists to the medium, Lawrence, and others like her, design and weave their tapestries themselves. She draws, paints and takes photographs, and it is from this bank of images that she selects what will work on the very different scale of the loom.

Kay Lawrence's work as a textile artist working in tapestry has developed considerably since her studies in the medium at the Edinburgh College of Art in 1977–78. From her base in South Australia, where she also teaches at the University of South Australia, she has produced numerous tapestries, many drawing on landscape and, some, more recently, on relationships, notably those between mother and daughter. Several of her tapestry projects, like the Parliament House Embroidery, have been community projects, consistent with her commitment to the communal and educative role of art, and also in keeping with the long-established practice of teamwork when tackling the painstakingly slow processes peculiar to many textile arts.

a walk around on the inside looking out
(detail)
1980-81

Kay Lawrence is well respected as a practitioner and teacher in Australia. Her work has been included in numerous exhibitions, both here and overseas, and is represented in several public art museum collections in Australia. In 1997, I had the rare pleasure of cutting down one of her tapestries, 'Daughter', from the loom upon its completion. 'Daughter' has an image, derived from a photograph taken by Lawrence of her own daughter, superimposed on a text. In addition to the mother–daughter relationship, she explores the idea of capturing the transitory in a medium that is the antithesis of spontaneous expression.

'Daughter' was commissioned by the Art Gallery of South Australia, Adelaide, an appropriate acquisition for a collection that possesses the finest tapestry in Australia, Morris & Co.'s 'Adoration of the Magi' (1900-02). Over one hundred and ten years ago William Morris wrote that the *noblest of the weaving arts is tapestry*, but he also wrote with characteristic bluntness: *...if a chap can't compose an epic poem while he's weaving a tapestry he had better shut up.* How pleased he would be to know that the tradition he revivified in the third quarter of the nineteenth century flourishes in Australia in the twenty-first.

right:
Daughter
1995-6
woven tapestry
cotton warp, linen, wool and cotton weft
194 x 141cm (76 x 56in)
The University of South Australia

Christopher Menz
Senior Curator, Decorative Arts
(International)
National Gallery of Victoria, NSW,
Australia

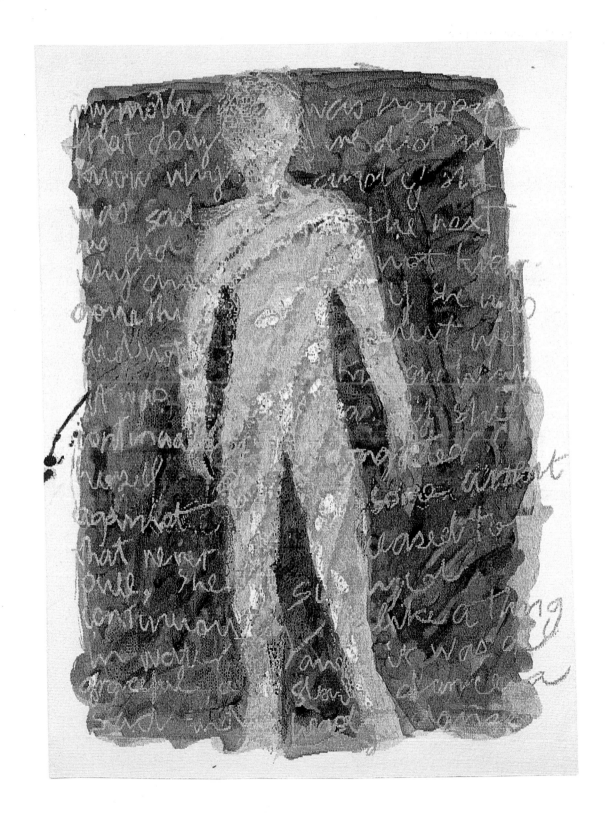

From Italowie to Chambers Gorge (detail)

1991-2

Kay Lawrence:
land, self, loss

A Gorgon in the mid-threads of a shawl, fringed with serpents is the description of a baby's shawl, the key motif of the story of the mythical Greek Kreusa. Raped by Apollo, the young princess hid their baby Ion in a cave at birth, wrapped in a covering woven with a Gorgon head she had made herself. His later recognition as a grown man, her son, by a distraught Kreusa depended on the identification of these figured cloths that she had woven as a girl. On this distinctive evidence which gave Ion his genealogical birthright hung the future of the people of Athens who were descended from him. The fierce Gorgon image, which originally had turned all viewers to stone, acted as an apotropaic ['turning away evil'] force to protect the innocent baby. Tapestries and woven images are crucial in Euripides' play in defining the architectural and political spaces in the Greek story of Ion as well as the understanding of personal fate.

Underpinning Kay Lawrence's work is an insistence on negotiating between the traditional techniques of woven Gobelin tapestry – so beautiful, laborious and persuasive – and the emergence of non-traditional and sometimes *subversive* approaches to the history of Australian settlement, in the positioning of women,

Aborigines and the environment. Her perception has moved through images of sparsely graphic landscapes in the 1980s commissioned for significant public and political spaces, towards the interior terrains of that most primal landscape, the family, since the 1990s.

Born in 1947 in Canberra, Kay Lawrence left Australia with her family when she was still a young child to live first in New Guinea, and later in Malaysia. Although her mother was born in Australia, her father had been born in Wales and his parents had emigrated from Wales in the 1920s to a remote town, Oodnadatta in South Australia to work on the railway. Her father was able to train as a meteorologist when he returned from World War II. After Malaysia her family returned to Adelaide, and Kay completed the Diploma of Art at the South Australian School of Art with an emphasis on painting and printmaking. Her mother died in 1970 after a long illness while only in her mid forties, and this event reverberates through Kay Lawrence's mature work.

Votes for Women
(detail of 'Centenary of Women's Suffrage Community Tapestries') 1993-4

A wave of excitement about the new possibilities of craft mediums had flowed to Australia in the mid 1960s. A ripple of such provocative new approaches to traditions of tapestry weaving was evident in the exquisite work of Belinda Ramson who had studied tapestry with the renowned Scottish weaver Archie Brennan in Scotland. Kay Lawrence attended summer schools in tapestry with her in South Australia in 1974 and 1975, choosing tapestry almost by accident.

Her interest in the medium was confirmed when she attended a workshop given by Archie Brennan when he visited Australia in 1976. Brennan had been the prime mover in elevating tapestry at Edinburgh as a revitalised medium commenting on popular culture and the intricacies of modern life with wit and elegance. He had also advised on the development of the influential Victorian Tapestry Workshop, set up in Melbourne in 1976 with State Government funding. Kay Lawrence travelled to Scotland in 1977 to study tapestry weaving with Maureen Hodge, Archie Brennan's successor at the Edinburgh College of Art, returning to South Australia in 1978 when the craft movement was blossoming.

Two Years, Two Hills (detail)
1982-3

a walk around on the inside looking out
1980-81
woven tapestry,
cotton warp, wool, cotton and linen weft
110 x 448cm (43 x 176in)
The Queensland Art Gallery, Australia

A woman's view: national identities

The substantial work 'a walk around on the inside looking out' foreshadows many later preoccupations. Here, a woman's view is strongly indicated, where the outer landscape is mediated through the window framework and glass reflections. A dark interior with light outside is repeated in the five panels that form a long narrative. Although the tapestry's formal strength relates to the imagery of mainstream artists, the difference lies in the crafted medium and the reference to the feminine viewpoint of 'inside looking out' which connects Lawrence's work to often hidden domestic histories.

The continued reflection and fascination with domestic artefacts is evident in the three small tapestries 'Rust' made twenty years later. [1] Lawrence's still life objects, prefigured by the milk bottle in 'a walk around the inside looking out' are like emblems of ourselves weathered by the archaeology of our lives. The primacy of drawing in her images separates her tapestries from the structural emphasis on material found in the textile art of the pervasive 'fibrearts' movement.
Another meditation on the divided

light and dark image followed in the tapestry 'Two Years, Two Hills'. The representation of the Australian bush landscape in the first half of the twentieth century had been very much a masculine domain, where virility and strength were the qualities underlying the settlement of the land. Although some women artists, for example Hilda Rix Nicholas, had struggled to make the experience of the bush of equal importance from a woman's perspective, the vast spaces of the arid inland were famously mythologised in the 1940s, 50s and 60s by Russell Drysdale, Arthur Boyd and Sydney Nolan and given iconic form in the paintings of Fred Williams.

'Two Years, Two Hills' nods to these stylistic influences in the depiction of a modern landscape, but the hills are seen not as the space for heroic or mythic action but as two light and dark symbols of a feminine psyche, one in South Australia, one in Dartmoor in England, which were *bound up with my emotional life*. [2] Both 'a walk around on the inside looking out' and 'Two Years, Two Hills' have an imagery characterised by an energetic diagonal mark, which is both abstract and representational of the scribbled vegetation of the stark hills of South Australia.

Two Years, Two Hills
1982-3
woven tapestry
cotton warp, wool, cotton and linen weft
246 x 337cm (96 x 133in)
Collection of the Commonwealth of Australia

The inclusion of fossil forms in 'Two Years, Two Hills' overlaid the brief personal time noted in the title with the immeasurably ancient layers of the landscape. The depth and complexity of the Australian landscape in which European settlement is such a brief moment, are indicated by the Aboriginal petroglyphs depicted in the major tapestry 'Red Gorge, Two Views' commissioned for the Prime Minister's Suite in the new Parliament House in Canberra. Such references within a landscape subtly underlined the fact that the exclusion of Aboriginal viewpoints and understanding of land had become a political issue in the celebration of two hundred years of European settlement in 1988.

The underlying issues of reconciliation between the two cultures are revisited in the recent tapestry 'Translation' [3] extending the meditations foreshadowed in 'Red Gorge, Two Views'. New anxieties have emerged in the wide debate about Aboriginal reconciliation and European occupation of Australia. The gridded field of pale golds and ochres is an interpretation of dyes from the native plants of Lake Mungo named in both English and the Paakantyi Aboriginal tongue.

Translation (detail)
1999-2000

Red Gorge, Two Views

1987-8

woven tapestry, cotton warp, wool, cotton and linen weft

193 x 359cm (76 x 141in)

woven by Kay Lawrence, Jude Stewart, Chris Cocius, and Shirley Benlow,

with additional assistance from Sue Rosenthal.

Parliament House, Canberra

Another complex desert 'Gorge' tapestry 'From Italowie to Chambers Gorge' subtly recording the changes European settlement made to the land, was commissioned for the Sembler Building in Florida, USA. Viewed from close up, this densely detailed and poetic work is an intricate mosaic of flecks of colour that take on an illusionary realism from further away. The bromide cartoon, enlarged from original landscape photographs, is translated almost magically into tiny woven units.

This Sembler commission emphasised the architectural role of tapestry. Both textiles and tapestry have been distinct from other artforms in acknowledging a collaborative basis in the workshop, between designer, weaver, architect, dyer and spinner. Kay Lawrence's energetic involvement as a teacher, and as a committee member for national arts organisations has emphasised the importance of generously collaborative models in public arts.

From Italowie to Chambers Gorge
1991-2
woven tapestry
cotton warp, wool, cotton and linen weft
122 x 478cm (48 x 188in)
woven with assistance from Lucia Pichler
The Sembler Building, St Peterburg, Florida, USA

left:

Hungry Rabbits
Thackaringa,
1890 drought
(detail of 'The Parliament
House Embroidery')

next page:
The Parliament House Embroidery,
Canberra
1982-8
wool and cotton embroidery on linen cloth
65 x 1600cm (26 x 629in)
Designer: Kay Lawrence
Coordinator: Anne Richards
embroidered by the members
of Embroiderer's Guilds across Australia

The Parliament House Embroidery

.....Manoo mamaa arganangam Wungudanjama arganangama

The desire of women's Embroiderer's Guilds throughout Australia to contribute to a sense of Australian history in the Bicenntenial year 1988, led by embroiderer Dorothy Hyslop, resulted in the monumental Parliament House Embroidery made as a gift to the nation and installed in a long glass case in the Great Hall. [4]

Kay Lawrence's concept was unanimously selected from an initial design competition in 1983. She emphasised in her design *land as a conditioner of values*. Her research, which indicated that the seemingly *natural* landscape had been deeply altered by human intervention, by *European agriculture and buildings, displacement of indigenous plants and animals*, led to a sometimes controversial use of imagery. The embroidery begins with a harmonious Aboriginal image of land followed by European maps leading to images of the hardships and difficulty of the pioneers clearing the land, building houses, suffering plagues of rabbits, bushfires and drought. The embroidery ends with an image of land that refers back to the beginning, suggesting *a growing awareness of our responsibility and an acknowledgement of our indebtedness to the land we have made ours.* [5]

Images derived from quilts, illustrations, maps, photographs and letters, as well Lawrence's own drawings of open hills or fire-blackened trees were combined in her design to bring together many layers of the Australian landscape. The complex assemblage of marks, lines, washes of colour and fine detail was skilfully and imaginatively interpreted in stitch on Glenshee linen twill, embroidered in sections by four hundred and ninety eight women from guilds all over Australia to form an extraordinary narrative, sixteen metres in length.

For this collaborative project, using *the landscape to express fundamental ideas about Australia*, Kay Lawrence was awarded the Order of Australia (AM).

The Women's Suffrage Centenary Tapestries

South Australia had been notable for its early support of the vote for women since 1884. Lawrence's passion for equity, for inclusion of women and Aboriginal people into the official history of the 'polis' informed the imagery of the two 'Women's Suffrage Centenary Tapestries' designed for the House of Assembly, South Australian Parliament.[6] The project to make the two tapestries, 'Women's suffrage: Votes for Women' representing nineteenth century legislation and 'Women's suffrage: Equal before the Law' representing twentieth century legislation, was initiated by two Liberal women politicians, Jennifer Cashmore and Diana Laidlaw. Kay Lawrence described the design process:

To structure the design I decided to use visual and written documentary evidence and images of artefacts – such as a child's embroidered sampler, a bride's wedding veil – which could be pieced together and juxtaposed in a collage, so connections could be made through reading one image against another... much as women pieced together quilts.

The two Suffrage tapestries, 'Votes for Women' and 'Equal before the Law' were made by community weavers coordinated by Elaine Gardner, assisted by Lucia Pichler, in an open and accessible space in the heart of Adelaide during 1993-4. The presence of these two tapestries in the Parliament Chamber since 1994 *symbolically insert women into one of the most male dominated and conservative institutions in Australian culture, the Parliament.*[7] Tapestry is a powerful medium for the representation of *subversive* ideas because although it is linked to the power of the state in its European ancestry, its fabric is a textile, a sign of the anonymous feminine and the domestic. *It was these almost contradictory associations of tapestry and textiles... that I wanted to play off in my design for the tapestries,* wrote the artist.[8]

Women's Suffrage Sth Australia 1894

Centenary of Women's Suffrage Community Tapestries
House of Assembly,
South Australian Parliament, Adelaide.
Two woven tapestries,1993-4
woven by the Adelaide Community
Weavers, coordinator Elaine Gardner,
assistant Lucia Pichler.

above:
Votes for Women
240 x 157cm (94 x 63in)

opposite:
Equal before the Law
240 x 192cm (94 x 76in)

Intimacy and Gender

The impressive public aspects of Lawrence's activity as an artist have a counterpoint in the almost searingly inward tapestries of the 1990s.

The surprising aspect of the tapestry exhibition 'Texts from the Edge: tapestry and identity in Australia' in 1995 was the preoccupation among many of the artists with sexual boundaries and ambiguities. The importance of textiles as a repressed artform in the west, had been opened up by Griselda Pollock and Rozsika Parker.[9] Another strong influence were French feminists such as Julia Kristeva, Helene Cixous and Luce Iragaray who investigated the formation of subjectivity in relation to women's creativity. [10]

Kay Lawrence's own words indicate the *edginess* of her position. *My practice in woven tapestry and drawing is on the edge of both the visual arts and crafts, informed by the long tradition of woven tapestry ... yet engaged in negotiating issues like feminism, representation and identity. The contradictions and tensions that arise from working at this edge invite questions rather than answers. It is these uncertainties that activate my work.*[11]

The relationship between the outer world of nature, so richly explored in Lawrence's works of the 1980s, and the inner world of self is one of these edges in contemporary thinking. According to Aristotle, nature (or Greek *physis* from *physein*, to be born) is the primary material element from which things that are born generate.[12] The power of generation and birth is located in the mother who may also decide not to give birth or nurture the young. The Greek myth of Demeter taught that when her daughter was torn away, the earth withered. Nature stopped when Demeter lost Persephone.

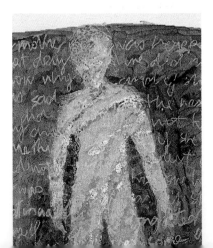

Daughter
1995-6
woven tapestry
cotton warp, linen, wool and cotton weft
194 x 141cm (76 x 56in)
The University of South Australia

Gender tapestry
(detail)
1993

This fundamental connection between mother and daughter has been the subject of a series of tapestries by Kay Lawrence, represented here by 'Gender' and 'Daughter'. The emphasis on the matrilineal line in Lawrence's work reflects the tenuousness of 'woman as artist', the difficulty of positioning another order of perception beside the historical masculine emphasis of Australian art. Often this other order may reflect an androgynous view where the boundaries between genders become increasingly blurred. Such androgyny is seen in the 'Gender' tapestry, which shows her eight year old daughter's exploratory drawings of the problematic issue of sexual identity. [13]

The importance of text in the textile (both derived from the Latin *texere* to weave) resonates in the elegiac colours of the 'Daughter' tapestry where a handwritten text streams across the background to the figure: *My mother was happy that day we did not know why and if she was sad the next we did not know why...* Against the indeterminate character of the mother in the text, the daughter hovers as a shadowy neutral silhouette. Although the drawn image is of her own daughter, it could as well be the artist as daughter held within the flowing handwritten text that describes the lost mother who went too early and too little known.

Gender tapestry

1993

woven tapestry

cotton warp, linen, wool and cotton weft

139 x 157cm (55 x 62in)

right:

Daughter (detail)

1995-6

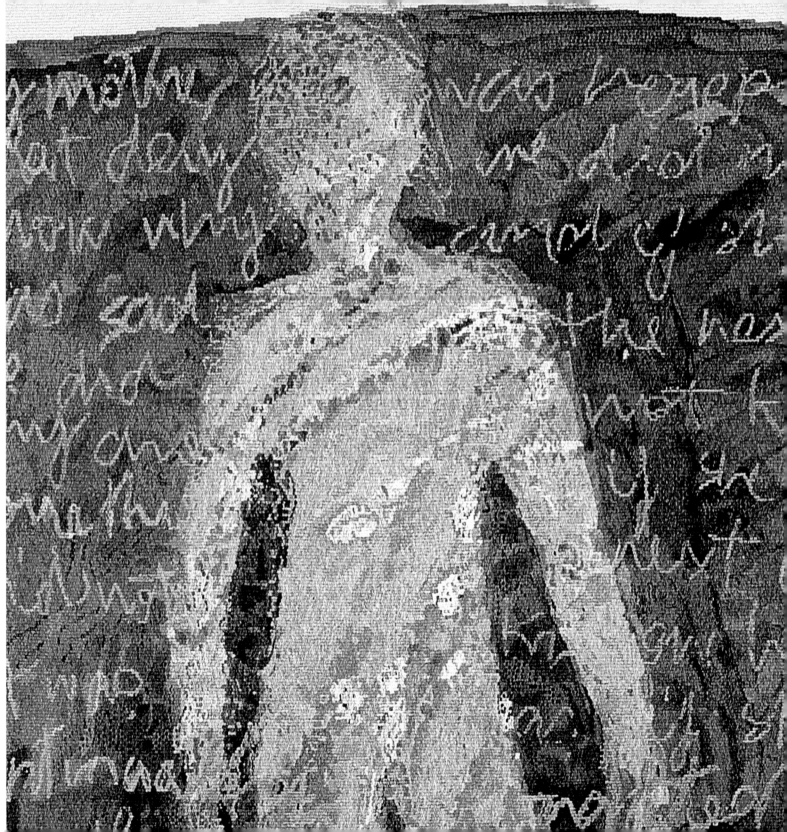

This vivid graphic text around the figure is simultaneously script, image and textile, reminding us that the very process of making a tapestry is like writing a narrative, building up the story in a consecutive chain of connection. The word for thread, and the line that draws both text and image have a common origin in the Latin root *lino*, meaning linen or flax.[14] The image of the daughter flickers against the current of barely discernible words, whose velocity seems to threaten the boundaries of her body.

Psychiatry has questioned the idea of the human body/psyche as an integrated *vessel*, describing the body as fragmented and even pierced with holes. The series 'Spill' has twenty one small tapestries of iconic funnels and sieves.[15] The sieve was a symbol of chastity in the Roman legend of the Vestal Virgin, Tuccia. *Vessels that leak* wrote Kay Lawrence, *like the sieve, can play on our anxieties about the dissolution of identity and suggest the impossiblity of maintaining a permanently fixed and stable sense of self.*[16]

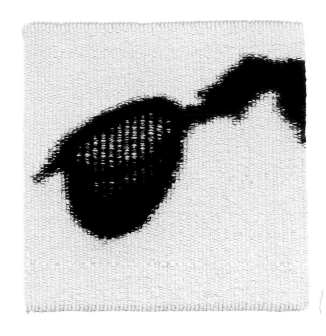

Spill
(details)
1997-98
woven tapestry
cotton warp, linen, wool and cotton weft
18 x 18cm (7 x 7in)

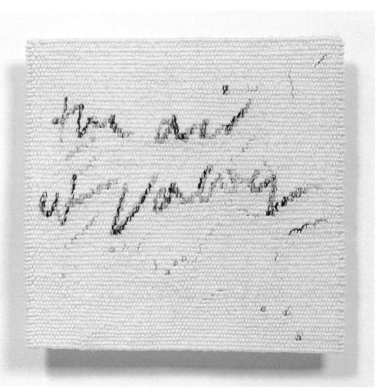

Spill

1997-98

woven tapestry, cotton warp, linen, wool and cotton weft

21 tapestries, each 18 x 18cm (7 x 7in)

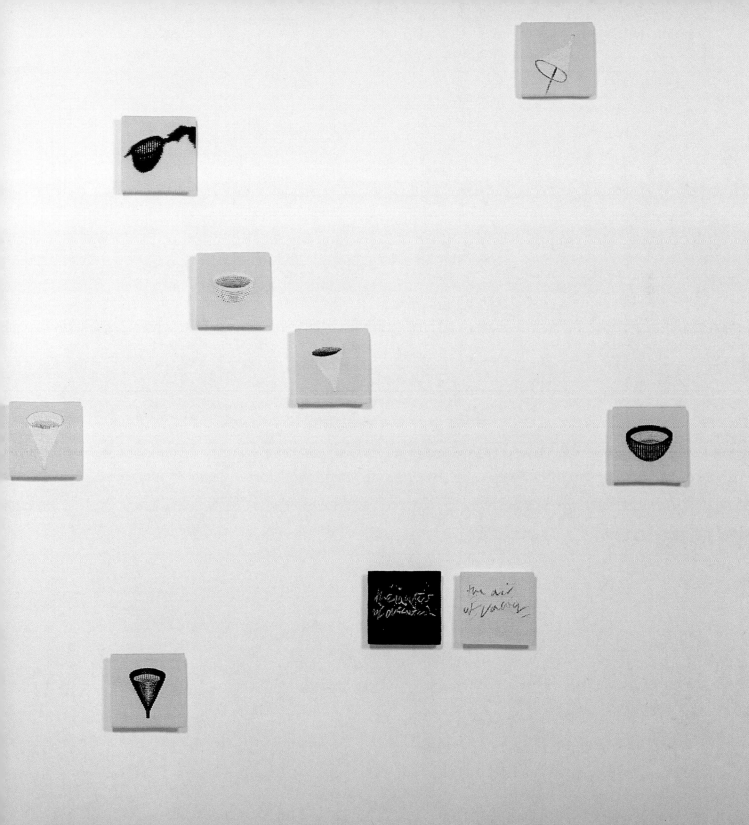

The 1999 tapestry 'Waiting' [17] with its dark image derived from an unfocused photograph expresses the uncertainty of adolescence. As in 'Daughter', the strong iconic image is without clear features, a brooding sphinx-like silhouette, where unusually for Lawrence, there are no sharp lines. Instead of graphic edges there is a blur between figure and ground.

Two small skulls accompanied the 'Waiting' tapestry ('Head of Death' & 'Purple Skull') like protective monsters at the edge of consciousness, apotropaic gorgons which ward off the forces of disintegration. In ancient Greek thought *eros*, the force of love and fertility was always linked to *thanatos*, death; though the representation of the death's heads in these skulls is derived from an adolescent drawing and the medieval 'Apocalypse tapestry' from Angers.

It is fitting to talk about Kay Lawrence's compelling imagery in relation to classical myth both because of the antiquity of the tapestry medium in European history, and its long involvement with narratives and texts which define and give identity to culture and self. Historically, she is one of a generation of artists who were told as students that there are no great women artists, and whose work provides a continuous questioning of seemingly fixed and impermeable male and female identities.

The woven Gorgon image of the Greek myth represented a monstrous face fringed with serpents. Such an image showed the *unseemly* aspect of the feminine which protected the vulnerable across society, and linked textiles to the generative female and the forces of the earth. Similarly in Kay Lawrence's deeply considered body of work the trauma of loss is averted by the tight woven structure of tapestry, the metaphor of the unified fabric of both self and society.

Dr Diana Wood Conroy
Associate Professor
Faculty of Creative Arts
University of Wollongong, NSW

Purple Skull
1997
woven tapestry
cotton warp, linen, wool
and cotton weft
27 x 18cm (11 x 7in)

Footnotes

AS Way (trans) 'Ion', in *Euripedes: Plays*. JM Dent & Sons Limited, New York and London, 1956, pp151-199, Marina Warner *Monuments and Maidens: the Allegory of the Female Form*. Wedenfeld and Nicolson, London, 1985.

1   Made for 'Home is Where the Heart is'. Federation exhibition curated by Vivonne Thwaites, in association with the South Australian Country Women's Association, Adelaide, South Australia 2001.

2   Kay Lawrence, Letter to Diana Wood Conroy, 1998.

3   Made for 'Lake Mungo Revisited' Goulburn Regional Art Gallery. Curator, Jennifer Lamb. Catalogue published by Goulburn Regional Gallery and the University of Wollongong, NSW, Australia 2000.

4   Kay Lawrence 'The Design', *The Parliament House Embroidery: A work of many hands*. Australian Government Publishing Service, Canberra, 1988, pp. 6-11.

5   *The Parliament House Embroidery: A work of many hands*. See also Grace Cochrane. A History of the Crafts Movement in Australia, University of Technology Press, Sydney, 1992.

6   Sue Rowley, 'Kay Lawrence'. Catalogue, *Crossing Borders: Contemporary Australian Textile Art*. University of Wollongong, 1995, pp. 60-61.

7   Kay Lawrence. Unpublished paper for 'Artist's Forum', Canberra School of Art, 1995.

8   *Texts from the Edge. Tapestry and Identity in Australia*.

9   Griselda Pollock and Rozsika Parker *Old Mistresses: Women, Art and Ideology*, Routledge and Kegan Paul, London, 1981 *The Subversive Stitch: Embroidery and the making of the feminine*. London, 1984 *Framing Feminism: Art and the Women's Movement 1970-1985*, Pandora. London and New York, 1987.

10   Toril Moi *Sexual/Textural politics: Feminist Literary Theory*, Methuen. London and New York, 1985.

11   Glenda King. *Origins and New Perspectives: Contemporary Australian Textiles*. Catalogue for exhibition at Lödz, Poland. Queen Victoria Museum and Art Gallery, Tasmania and Craft Australia, Surrey Hills, Australia 1998, pp. 48-49.

12   Adriana Cavarero translated by Serena Anderlini-D'Onofrio and Aine O'Healy. *In spite of Plato: A feminist re-writing of ancient philosophy*, Polity Press with Blackwell Publishers, Oxford, 1995.

13   Catalogue *Identities: Art from Australia*, Taipei Fine Arts Museum, Taiwan, December 1993 - February 1994, pp. 97-99.

14   J Hillis Miller. *Ariadne's Thread: Story Lines*. Yale University Press, New Haven and London 1992, pp. 6-7.

15   Anne Brennan 'Embodying and Spilling'. Catalogue essay, *Threefold: an exhibition in three parts for 'Shift'*. Canberra School of Art, 1990.
Diana Wood Conroy: 'Oblivion and Metamorphosis: Australian weavers in relation to ancient artefacts from Cyprus'. Sue Rowley (ed) *Re-inventing Textiles, vol 1 Tradition and Innovation*. Telos Art Publishing, Winchester, 1999, pp. 21-31.

16   Kay Lawrence. Letters to Diana Wood Conroy, 1998.

17   first exhibited in the exhibition 'Close Ties: Kay Lawrence and Marcel Marois'. Catalogue, The University of Queensland Art Museum, curated by Ruth McDougall. The University of Queensland, 1999.

THUJ KURU · PANPA · THURPA · ROSEWOOD · · PINPA · MURRAY PIN

KURU · KIRA · BOX GUM · THAPI · NHIIIYI · MISTLETOE

Biography

Born	1947, Australia

Education

1977 - 1978	Edinburgh College of Art, Scotland (Tapestry weaving)
1965 - 1968	Dip Art Teaching with Postgraduate Year in Painting and Printmaking

Professional

2002 -	Head, South Australian School of Art, University of South Australia
2001 -	Portfolio Leader of Research, South Australian School of Art, Uni SA
1995 - 2000	Senior Lecturer and Co-ordinator, Textiles Studios, Uni SA
1998 - 2000	President, Craftsouth
1997	Joint Coordinator, 'Lake Mungo Project' (international artists' retreat)
1996 - 1997	Board, Crafts Council of South Australia
1990 - 1992	Organiser, 'Distant Lives/Shared Voices', symposium on woven tapestry, Lödz, Poland
1994 - 1995	Joint Curator & Co-ordinator, 'Texts from the Edge, Tapestry & Identity in Australia' (touring exhibition & symposium)
1971 - 1994	Lecturer: Painting, Printmaking, Sculpture, South Australian School of Art, Uni SA
1989 - 1991	Chair, 'Art for Public Places' Committee, South Australia
1985 - 1989	Member of the Visual Arts/Craft Board of the Australia Council
1984	Member of the Arts Grant Advisory Panel, Government of South Australia

Artist in Community

1999 - 2001	Coordinator, Barbara Hanrahan Community Tapestry Project
1993	Designs for the Women's Suffrage Centenary Community Tapestries, South Australian Parliament
1989	Designer, Community Tapestry, Regency Park Centre for the Young Disabled
1984/85	Millicent Community Tapestry
1983	Crafers School Tapestry
1982/83	Hills Community Tapestry
1981	Salisbury Community Tapestry

Rust

2001

three woven tapestries

cotton warp, linen,wool and cotton weft

each 45 x 37cm (18 x 15in)

Selected Commissions

2001	'Weaving the Murray', The Centenary of Federation, SA (with Rhonda Agius, Nici Cumpston, Kirsty Darlaston, Sandy Elverd, Chrissie Houston, Karen Russell)
1995 - 1996	'Daughter', Art Gallery of South Australia
1990 - 1992	'From Italowie to Chambers Gorge', The Sembler Building, St Petersburg, Florida, USA
1987 - 1988	'Red Gorge, Two Views', Prime Minister's Suite in Parliament House, Canberra
1984 - 1986	Designer: 'The Parliament House Embroidery'
1982	'Two Years, Two Hills', Australian High Commission in Dhaka, Bangladesh

Selected Grants and Awards

2000	Visiting Scholar, Goldsmiths College, University of London, England
1998	HC Coombs Creative Arts Fellow, Australian National University
1996,1997,1998	Australian Research Council Grants: 'Significant Women Artists at the S. Australian School of Art'
1996	Fellowship, Visual Arts/Craft Fund, Australia Council
1992	Artist's Development Grant to attend 'Distant Lives, Shared Voices', Lödz, Poland
1989	Member of the Order of Australia (AM) for service to the arts

Solo and Two-person Exhibitions

1999	'Close Ties, Kay Lawrence & Marcel Marois', University of Queensland Art Museum (tour)
1985	Installation of Paperworks, Lessness Festival Theatre Gallery, Adelaide
1981	Exhibition of drawings and tapestries, Jam Factory Gallery, Adelaide

Selected Writing

2001	*Voyage: Home is where we start from*, illustrated correspondence with Lindsay Obermeyer in *Reinventing Textiles, vol 2, Gender & Identity,* Ed Prof. Janis Jefferies, Telos Art Publishing, Winchester
2000	Catalogue essay on Elsje van Keppel in *The Return of Beauty*, Adelaide Festival Exhibition, Jam Factory.
1999	*Losing and Finding, Loss and Reparation*, Fiberarts (Summer)
1998	*Memory and Materiality*, Australian representation at the 9th Triennale of Tapestry Poland *Origins and New perspectives* catalogue
1997	*Fragile Objects by Elsje King*, Object, 1997 No 2
1995	Editor, essay on Marie Cook, *Texts from the Edge* catalogue
1995	*Gender and the Practice of Textiles*, Australian Art Education, Vol 18 no 2 1995

Selected Group Exhibitions

2001	'Home is where the Heart is', Burra Regional Gallery South Australia (tour)
2000	'Chemistry', Art Gallery of South Australia
2000	'Lake Mungo Revisited', Goulburn Regional Art Gallery, Goulburn (tour)
2000	'Frisson 13th Tamworth Textile Biennale', Tamworth City Gallery (tour)
1999	'Drawn in Form', Brisbane City Art Gallery
1998	'Threefold. Elsje van Keppel, Kay Lawrence, Ernabella Arts', Canberra School of Art Gallery, ANU
1998	'Origins and New Perspectives, Contemporary Australian Textiles', Lödz Poland
1997	'A response to Lake Mungo, Works in progress', Long Gallery University of Wollongong
1995 - 97	'Crossing Borders Contemporary Australian Textiles Art' (tour USA)
1994 - 95	'Texts from the Edge, Tapestry & Identity', Jam Factory, Adelaide (tour)
1993 - 94	'Identities, Art from Australia', Taipeh Fine Arts Museum, Taiwan
1991	'Asia Pacific Crafts Exhibition', Kyoto, Japan
1989 - 91	'Makers Choice', Adelaide Festival Centre (tour)
1988	'World Tapestry Today', American Tapestry Alliance, Melbourne
1986	'Fremantle Drawing Prize', Festival of Perth, Fremantle Arts Centre, Fremantle
1983	'Australian Paperworks', Kyoto, Japan
1981	'Maude Vizard-Wholohan Purchase Award', Art Gallery of South Australia
1981	'Lödz Textile Triennale', Poland
1981	'Batman Purchase', Exhibition, Queen Victoria Museum and Art Gallery, Launceston
1980	'Australian Weavers in Wool', Melbourne and London

Public Collections

The Australian National Gallery
The Queensland Art Gallery
The Art Gallery of South Australia
The Art Gallery of Western Australia
The Queen Victoria Museum and Art Gallery, Launceston, Tasmania
The Art Gallery of Tasmania, Hobart
Museum of Applied Arts and Sciences, NSW
New Parliament House, Canberra

the artist with

Waiting

1998-9

woven tapestry

cotton warp, linen, wool and cotton weft

135 x 155cm

The University of South Australia

Other titles in this series

Vol 6: Anne Wilson
by Tim Porges and Hattie Gordon
This important American artist uses human
hair, table linens and hand-stitching to probe
poignant personal memories and histories,
as well as evoking a subtle sense of landscape.
ISBN 1 902015 22 3 (softback)

Vol 7: Alice Kettle (February 2003)
by Dr Jennifer Harris
Get up close and intimate with recent major
works by this Winchester-based painter who
has become one of the world's most popular
embroiderers.
ISBN 1 902015 31 2 (softback)
ISBN 1 902015 53 3 (hardback)

Vol 8: Helen Lancaster (April 2002)
by Carolynne Skinner
The perilous fragility of nature, beautifully
depicted by an outstanding conceptual
environmentalist using paint, crochet,
embroidery and fabric manipulation.
ISBN 1 902015 29 0 (softback)
ISBN 1 902015 45 2 (hardback)

Vol 9: Kay Lawrence (April 2002)
by Dr Diana Wood Conroy
One of the world's top tapestry weavers, her
recent work negotiates issues about identity
in textures ranging from minimal to lush,
from sensuous to spiky.
ISBN 1 902015 28 2 (softback)
ISBN 1 902015 44 4 (hardback)

Vol 10: Joan Livingstone (April 2002)
by Gerry Craig
Livingstone's powerful installations incorpo-
rate felt, stitch and epoxy resin. Professor of
Fiber and Material Studies in Chicago, she is
one of America's most important sculptors.
ISBN 1 902015 27 4 (softback)
ISBN 1 902015 43 6 (hardback)

Vol 11: Marian Smit (April 2002)
by Marjolein v.d. Stoep
1st Prize winner in Third International Paper Triennal,
Switzerland, 1999. "Work of great simplicity
combining technique and poetry."
ISBN 1 902015 32 0 (softback)
ISBN 1 902015 46 0 (hardback)

Vol 12: Chiyoko Tanaka (April 2002)
by Lesley Millar
Tanaka's prized weavings are in public collections
around the world. A leading light from Kyoto,
her work is breathtaking and awe-inspiring.
ISBN 1 902015 24 X (softback)
ISBN 1 902015 42 8 (hardback)

Volume 14: Lia Cook (September 2002)
by Jenni Sorkin
Lia Cook's provocative weavings combine aspects
of digital technology, painting and photography.
Referencing diverse art histories, her images are distilled
from a seemingly random movement of threads.
ISBN 1 902015 34 7 (softback)
ISBN 1 902015 51 7 (hardback)

Volume 15: Jane Lackey (September 2002)
by Irena Hofmann and Helga Pakasaar
Artist-in-residence at Cranbrook Academy of Art, her
sculptural objects, installations and prints offer beguiling
contemplations on the patterns, codes and maps of
information concealed within the body.
ISBN 1 902015 35 5 (softback)
ISBN 1 902515 52 5 (hardback)

**Please visit our website for details of all
other volumes in this growing series.
www.arttextiles.com**